MW00616308

The
Geographical
Pivot of
History

The Geographical Pivot of History

SIR HALFORD MACKINDER

COSIMOCLASSICS

NEW YORK

The Geographical Pivot of History
First published in *The Geographical Journal* in 1904.
Current edition published by Cosimo Clasics in 2019.

ISBN: 978-1-94593-481-0 (pb); ISBN: 978-1-64679-661-8 (hc)

This edition is a classic text and may be considered rare. As such, it is possible that some of the text might be blurred or of reduced print quality. Thank you for your understanding and we wish you a pleasant reading experience.

Cosimo aims to publish books that inspire, inform, and engage readers worldwide. We use innovative print-on-demand technology that enables books to be printed based on specific customer needs. This approach eliminates an artificial scarcity of publications and allows us to distribute books in the most efficient and environmentally sustainable manner. Cosimo also works with printers and paper manufacturers who practice and encourage sustainable forest management, using paper that has been certified by the FSC, SFI, and PEFC whenever possible.

Ordering Information:
Cosimo publications are available at online bookstores. They may also be purchased for educational, business, or promotional use:
   Bulk orders: Special discounts are available on bulk orders for reading groups, organizations, businesses, and others.
   Custom-label orders: We offer selected books with your customized cover or logo of choice.

For more information, contact us at www.cosimobooks.com

The

Geographical Journal.

No. 4. APRIL, 1904. Vol. XXIII.

THE GEOGRAPHICAL PIVOT OF HISTORY.[*]

By H. J. MACKINDER, M.A., Reader in Geography in the University of
Oxford; Director of the London School of Economics and Political Science.

WHEN historians in the remote future come to look back on the group
of centuries through which we are now passing, and see them fore-
shortened, as we to-day see the Egyptian dynasties, it may well be that
they will describe the last 400 years as the Columbian epoch, and will say
that it ended soon after the year 1900. Of late it has been a common-
place to speak of geographical exploration as nearly over, and it is recog-
nized that geography must be diverted to the purpose of intensive survey
and philosophic synthesis. In 400 years the outline of the map of the
world has been completed with approximate accuracy, and even in the
polar regions the voyages of Nansen and Scott have very narrowly
reduced the last possibility of dramatic discoveries. But the opening
of the twentieth century is appropriate as the end of a great historic
epoch, not merely on account of this achievement, great though it be.
The missionary, the conqueror, the farmer, the miner, and, of late, the
engineer, have followed so closely in the traveller's footsteps that the
world, in its remoter borders, has hardly been revealed before we must
chronicle its virtually complete political appropriation. In Europe,
North America, South America, Africa, and Australasia there is
scarcely a region left for the pegging out of a claim of ownership,
unless as the result of a war between civilized or half-civilized powers.
Even in Asia we are probably witnessing the last moves of the game
first played by the horsemen of Yermak the Cossack and the shipmen
of Vasco da Gama. Broadly speaking, we may contrast the Columbian
epoch with the age which preceded it, by describing its essential

* Read at the Royal Geographical Society, January 25, 1904.

characteristic as the expansion of Europe against almost negligible resistances, whereas mediæval Christendom was pent into a narrow region and threatened by external barbarism. From the present time forth, in the post-Columbian age, we shall again have to deal with a closed political system, and none the less that it will be one of world-wide scope. Every explosion of social forces, instead of being dissipated in a surrounding circuit of unknown space and barbaric chaos, will be sharply re-echoed from the far side of the globe, and weak elements in the political and economic organism of the world will be shattered in consequence. There is a vast difference of effect in the fall of a shell into an earthwork and its fall amid the closed spaces and rigid structures of a great building or ship. Probably some half-conscious-ness of this fact is at last diverting much of the attention of statesmen in all parts of the world from territorial expansion to the struggle for relative efficiency.

It appears to me, therefore, that in the present decade we are for the first time in a position to attempt, with some degree of completeness, a correlation between the larger geographical and the larger historical generalizations. For the first time we can perceive something of the real proportion of features and events on the stage of the whole world, and may seek a formula which shall express certain aspects, at any rate, of geographical causation in universal history. If we are fortunate, that formula should have a practical value as setting into perspective some of the competing forces in current international politics. The familiar phrase about the westward march of empire is an empirical and frag-mentary attempt of the kind. I propose this evening describing those physical features of the world which I believe to have been most coercive of human action, and presenting some of the chief phases of history as organically connected with them, even in the ages when they were unknown to geography. My aim will not be to discuss the influence of this or that kind of feature, or yet to make a study in regional geo-graphy, but rather to exhibit human history as part of the life of the world organism. I recognize that I can only arrive at one aspect of the truth, and I have no wish to stray into excessive materialism. Man and not nature initiates, but nature in large measure controls. My concern is with the general physical control, rather than the causes of universal history. It is obvious that only a first approximation to truth can be hoped for. I shall be humble to my critics.

The late Prof. Freeman held that the only history which counts is that of the Mediterranean and European races. In a sense, of course, this is true, for it is among these races that have originated the ideas which have rendered the inheritors of Greece and Rome dominant throughout the world. In another and very important sense, however, such a limitation has a cramping effect upon thought. The ideas which go to form a nation, as opposed to a mere crowd of human animals,

have usually been accepted under the pressure of a common tribu-
lation, and under a common necessity of resistance to external force.
The idea of England was beaten into the Heptarchy by Danish and
Norman conquerors; the idea of France was forced upon competing
Franks, Goths, and Romans by the Huns at Chalons, and in the
Hundred Years' War with England; the idea of Christendom was born
of the Roman persecutions, and matured by the Crusades; the idea of the
United States was accepted, and local colonial patriotism sunk, only in
the long War of Independence; the idea of the German Empire was
reluctantly adopted in South Germany only after a struggle against
France in comradeship with North Germany.   What I may describe as
the literary conception of history, by concentrating attention upon ideas
and upon the civilization which is their outcome, is apt to lose sight of
the more elemental movements whose pressure is commonly the exciting
cause of the efforts in which great ideas are nourished.   A repellent
personality performs a valuable social function in uniting his enemies,
and it was under the pressure of external barbarism that Europe
achieved her civilization.   I ask you, therefore, for a moment to look
upon Europe and European history as subordinate to Asia and Asiatic
history, for European civilization is, in a very real sense, the outcome of
the secular struggle against Asiatic invasion.

The most remarkable contrast in the political map of modern
Europe is that presented by the vast area of Russia occupying half
the Continent and the group of smaller territories tenanted by the
Western Powers.   From a physical point of view, there is, of course,
a like contrast between the unbroken lowland of the east and the
rich complex of mountains and valleys, islands and peninsulas, which
together form the remainder of this part of the world.   At first sight
it would appear that in these familiar facts we have a correlation
between natural environment and political organization so obvious as
hardly to be worthy of description, especially when we note that
throughout the Russian plain a cold winter is opposed to a hot summer,
and the conditions of human existence thus rendered additionally
uniform.   Yet a series of historical maps, such as that contained in
the Oxford Atlas, will reveal the fact that not merely is the rough
coincidence of European Russia with the Eastern Plain of Europe a
matter of the last hundred years or so, but that in all earlier time
there was persistent re-assertion of quite another tendency in the
political grouping.   Two groups of states usually divided the country
into northern and southern political systems.   The fact is that
the orographical map does not express the particular physical contrast
which has until very lately controlled human movement and settlement
in Russia.   When the screen of winter snow fades northward off the
vast face of the plain, it is followed by rains whose maximum occurs
in May and June beside the Black sea, but near the Baltic and White

seas is deferred to July and August. In the south the later summer is a period of drought. As a consequence of this climatic *régime*, the north and north-west were forest broken only by marshes, whereas the south and south-east were a boundless grassy steppe, with trees only along the rivers. The line separating the two regions ran diagonally north-eastward from the northern end of the Carpathians

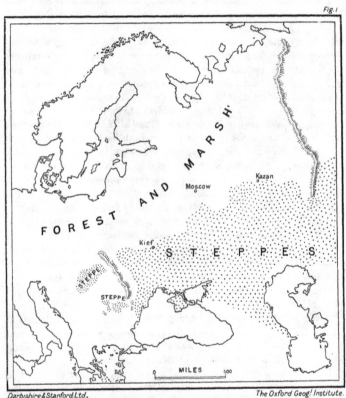

Fig. I

EASTERN EUROPE BEFORE THE 19TH CENTURY,
(AFTER DRUDE IN BERGHAUS' PHYSICAL ATLAS.)

to a point in the Ural range nearer to its southern than to its northern extremity. Moscow lies a little to north of this line, or, in other words, on the forest side of it. Outside Russia the boundary of the great forest ran westward almost exactly through the centre of the European isthmus, which is 800 miles across between the Baltic and the Black seas. Beyond this, in Peninsular Europe, the woods spread on through the plains of Germany in the north, while the steppe lands in the south

turned the great Transylvanian bastion of the Carpathians, and extended
up the Danube, through what are now the cornfields of Roumania, to the
Iron Gates. A detached area of steppes, known locally as Pusstas,
now largely cultivated, occupied the plain of Hungary, ingirt by the
forested rim of Carpathian and Alpine mountains. In all the west of
Russia, save in the far north, the clearing of the forests, the drainage of

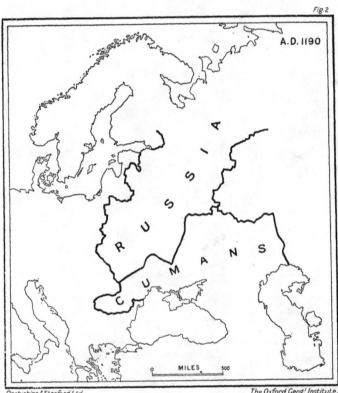

POLITICAL DIVISIONS OF EASTERN EUROPE
AT THE TIME OF THE 3ᴿᴰ CRUSADE,
(AFTER THE OXFORD HISTORICAL ATLAS)

the marshes, and the tillage of the steppes have recently averaged the
character of the landscape, and in large measure obliterated a distinction
which was formerly very coercive of humanity.

The earlier Russia and Poland were established wholly in the glades
of the forest. Through the steppe on the other hand there came from
the unknown recesses of Asia, by the gateway between the Ural mountains and the Caspian sea, in all the centuries from the fifth to the

sixteenth, a remarkable succession of Turanian nomadic peoples— Huns, Avars, Bulgarians, Magyars, Khazars, Patzinaks, Cumans, Mongols, Kalmuks. Under Attila the Huns established themselves in the midst of the Pusstas, in the uttermost Danubian outlier of the steppes, and thence dealt blows northward, westward, and southward against the settled peoples of Europe. A large part of modern

Fig. 3.

A.D. 1519

RUSSIA

SIBIR

KAZAN

POLAND

ASTRAKHAN

Zaporogian Cossacks

CRIMEA

OTTOMAN TURKS

Tartar & Turkish States

MILES
0   500

Darbishire & Stanford Ltd.   The Oxford Geog! Institute

**POLITICAL DIVISIONS OF EASTERN EUROPE
AT THE ACCESSION OF CHARLES V.**
(AFTER THE OXFORD HISTORICAL ATLAS.)

history might be written as a commentary upon the changes directly or indirectly ensuing from these raids. The Angles and Saxons, it is quite possible, were then driven to cross the seas to found England in Britain. The Franks, the Goths, and the Roman provincials were compelled, for the first time, to stand shoulder to shoulder on the battlefield of Chalons, making common cause against the Asiatics, who were unconsciously welding together modern France. Venice

was founded from the destruction of Aquileia and Padua; and even the
Papacy owed a decisive prestige to the successful mediation of Pope
Leo with Attila at Milan. Such was the harvest of results produced
by a cloud of ruthless and idealess horsemen sweeping over the un-
impeded plain—a blow, as it were, from the great Asiatic hammer
striking freely through the vacant space. The Huns were followed
by the Avars. It was for a marchland against these that Austria
was founded, and Vienna fortified, as the result of the campaigns
of Charlemagne. The Magyar came next, and by incessant raiding
from his steppe base in Hungary increased the significance of the
Austrian outpost, so drawing the political focus of Germany eastward to the margin of the realm. The Bulgarian established a ruling
caste south of the Danube, and has left his name upon the map,
although his language has yielded to that of his Slavonic subjects.
Perhaps the longest and most effective occupation of the Russian
steppe proper was that of the Khazars, who were contemporaries
of the great Saracen movement: the Arab geographers knew the
Caspian as the Khazar sea. In the end, however, new hordes arrived
from Mongolia, and for two centuries Russia in the northern forest
was held tributary to the Mongol Khans of Kipchak, or "the Steppe,"
and Russian development was thus delayed and biassed at a time when
the remainder of Europe was rapidly advancing.

It should be noted that the rivers running from the Forest to the
Black and Caspian seas cross the whole breadth of the steppe-land path
of the nomads, and that from time to time there were transient movements along their courses at right angles to the movement of the
horsemen. Thus the missionaries of Greek Christianity ascended the
Dnieper to Kief, just as beforehand the Norse Varangians had descended
the same river on their way to Constantinople. Still earlier, the
Teutonic Goths appear for a moment upon the Dniester, having crossed
Europe from the shores of the Baltic in the same south-eastward
direction. But these are passing episodes which do not invalidate the
broader generalization. For a thousand years a series of horse-riding
peoples emerged from Asia through the broad interval between the
Ural mountains and the Caspian sea, rode through the open spaces of
southern Russia, and struck home into Hungary in the very heart of
the European peninsula, shaping by the necessity of opposing them the
history of each of the great peoples around—the Russians, the Germans,
the French, the Italians, and the Byzantine Greeks. That they stimulated healthy and powerful reaction, instead of crushing opposition
under a widespread despotism, was due to the fact that the mobility of
their power was conditioned by the steppes, and necessarily ceased in
the surrounding forests and mountains.

A rival mobility of power was that of the Vikings in their boats.
Descending from Scandinavia both upon the northern and the southern

shores of Europe, they penetrated inland by the river ways. But the scope of their action was limited, for, broadly speaking, their power was effective only in the neighbourhood of the water. Thus the settled peoples of Europe lay gripped between two pressures—that of the Asiatic nomads from the east, and on the other three sides that of the pirates from the sea. From its very nature neither pressure was overwhelming, and both therefore were stimulative. It is noteworthy that the formative influence of the Scandinavians was second only in significance to that of the nomads, for under their attack both England and France made long moves towards unity, while the unity of Italy was broken by them. In earlier times, Rome had mobilized the power of her settled peoples by means of her roads, but the Roman roads had fallen into decay, and were not replaced until the eighteenth century.

It is likely that even the Hunnish invasion was by no means the first of the Asiatic series. The Scythians of the Homeric and Herodotian accounts, drinking the milk of mares, obviously practised the same arts of life, and were probably of the same race as the later inhabitants of the steppe. The Celtic element in the river-names *Don*, *Donetz*, *Dneiper*, *Dneister*, and *Danube* may possibly betoken the passage of peoples of similar habits, though not of identical race, but it is not unlikely that the Celts came merely from the northern forests, like the Goths and Varangians of a later time. The great wedge of population, however, which the anthropologists characterize as Brachy-Cephalic, driven westward from Brachy-Cephalic Asia through Central Europe into France, is apparently intrusive between the northern, western, and southern Dolico-Cephalic populations, and may very probably have been derived from Asia.[*]

The full meaning of Asiatic influence upon Europe is not, however, discernible until we come to the Mongol invasions of the fifteenth century; but before we analyze the essential facts concerning these, it is desirable to shift our geographical view-point from Europe, so that we may consider the Old World in its entirety. It is obvious that, since the rainfall is derived from the sea, the heart of the greatest land-mass is likely to be relatively dry. We are not, therefore, surprised to find that two-thirds of all the world's population is concentrated in relatively small areas along the margins of the great continent—in Europe, beside the Atlantic ocean; in the Indies and China, beside the Indian and Pacific oceans. A vast belt of almost uninhabited, because practically rainless, land extends as the Sahara completely across Northern Africa into Arabia. Central and Southern Africa were almost as completely severed from Europe and Asia throughout the greater part of history as were the Americas and Australia. In fact, the southern boundary of Europe was and is the Sahara rather than the

---

[*] See 'The Races of Europe,' by Prof. W. Z. Ripley (Kegan Paul, 1900).

Mediterranean, for it is the desert which divides the black man from the white. The continuous land-mass of Euro-Asia thus included between the ocean and the desert measures 21,000,000 square miles, or half of all the land on the globe, if we exclude from reckoning the deserts of Sahara and Arabia. There are many detached deserts scattered through Asia, from Syria and Persia north-eastward to Manchuria, but no such continuous vacancy as to be comparable with the Sahara. On the other hand, Euro-Asia is characterized by a very remarkable distribution of river drainage. Throughout an immense portion of the centre and north, the rivers have been practically useless for purposes of human communication with the outer world. The Volga, the Oxus, and the Jaxartes drain into salt lakes; the Obi, the Yenesei, and the Lena into the frozen ocean of the north. These are six of the

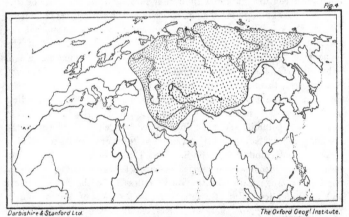

Fig. 4

Darbishire & Stanford Ltd.   *The Oxford Geog! Institute.*

CONTINENTAL AND ARCTIC DRAINAGE
EQUAL AREA PROJECTION

greatest rivers in the world. There are many smaller but still considerable streams in the same area, such as the Tarim and the Helmund, which similarly fail to reach the ocean. Thus the core of Euro-Asia, although mottled with desert patches, is on the whole a steppe-land supplying a wide-spread if often scanty pasture, and there are not a few river-fed oases in it, but it is wholly unpenetrated by waterways from the ocean. In other words, we have in this immense area all the conditions for the maintenance of a sparse, but in the aggregate considerable, population of horse-riding and camel-riding nomads. Their realm is limited northward by a broad belt of sub-arctic forest and marsh, wherein the climate is too rigorous, except at the eastern and western extremities, for the development of agricultural settlements. In the east the forests extend southward to the Pacific coast in the Amur land and Manchuria. Similarly in the west, in prehistoric Europe, forest was the predominant vegetation. Thus framed in to the north-east, north, and north-west, the steppes spread continuously for 4000 miles from the Pusstas of Hungary to the Little Gobi of Manchuria, and, except in their westernmost extremity, they are untraversed by rivers draining to an accessible ocean, for we may neglect the very recent efforts to trade to the mouths of the Obi and Yenisei. In Europe, Western Siberia, and Western Turkestan the steppe lands lie low, in some places below the level of the sea. Further to east, in Mongolia, they extend over plateaux; but the passage from the one level to the other, over the naked, unscarped lower ranges of the arid heart-land, presents little difficulty.

The hordes which ultimately fell upon Europe in the middle of the fourteenth century gathered their first force 3000 miles away on the high steppes of Mongolia. The havoc wrought for a few years in Poland, Silesia, Moravia, Hungary, Croatia, and Servia was, however, but the remotest and the most transient result of the great stirring of the nomads of the East associated with the name of Ghenghiz Khan. While the Golden Horde occupied the steppe of Kipchak, from the Sea of Aral, through the interval between the Ural range and the Caspian, to the foot of the Carpathians, another horde, descending south-westward between the Caspian sea and the Hindu Kush into Persia, Mesopotamia, and even into Syria, founded the domain of the Ilkhan. A third subsequently struck into Northern China, conquering Cathay. India and Mangi, or Southern China, were for a time shel-tered by the incomparable barrier of Tibet, to whose efficacy there is, perhaps, nothing similar in the world, unless it be the Sahara desert and the polar ice. But at a later time, in the days of Marco Polo in the case of Mangi, in those of Tamerlane in the case of India, the obstacle was circumvented. Thus it happened that in this typical and well-recorded instance, all the settled margins of the Old World sooner or later felt the expansive force of mobile power originating in the steppe. Russia, Persia, India, and China were either made tributary, or received Mongol dynasties. Even the incipient power of the Turks in Asia Minor was struck down for half a century.

As in the case of Europe, so in other marginal lands of Euro-Asia there are records of earlier invasions. China had more than once to submit to conquest from the north; India several times to conquest from the north-west. In the case of Persia, however, at least one of the earlier descents has a special significance in the history of Western civilization. Three or four centuries before the Mongols, the Seljuk Turks, emerging from Central Asia, overran by this path an immense area of the land, which we may describe as of the five seas—Caspian, Black, Mediterranean, Red, and Persian. They established themselves at Kerman, at Hamadan, and in Asia Minor, and they overthrew the

Saracen dominion of Bagdad and Damascus. It was ostensibly to punish their treatment of the Christian pilgrims at Jerusalem that Christendom undertook the great series of campaigns known collectively as the Crusades. Although these failed in their immediate objects, they so stirred and united Europe that we may count them as the beginning of modern history—another striking instance of European advance stimulated by the necessity of reacting against pressure from the heart of Asia.

The conception of Euro-Asia to which we thus attain is that of a continuous land, ice-girt in the north, water-girt elsewhere, measuring 21 million square miles, or more than three times the area of North America, whose centre and north, measuring some 9 million square miles, or more than twice the area of Europe, have no available water-ways to the ocean, but, on the other hand, except in the subarctic forest, are very generally favourable to the mobility of horsemen and camelmen. To east, south, and west of this heart-land are marginal regions, ranged in a vast crescent, accessible to shipmen. According to physical conformation, these regions are four in number, and it is not a little remarkable that in a general way they respectively coincide with the spheres of the four great religions—Buddhism, Brahminism, Mahometanism, and Christianity. The first two are the monsoon lands, turned the one towards the Pacific, and the other towards the Indian ocean. The fourth is Europe, watered by the Atlantic rains from the west. These three together, measuring less than 7 million square miles, have more than 1000 million people, or two-thirds of the world population. The third, coinciding with the land of the Five Seas, or, as it is more often described, the Nearer East, is in large measure deprived of moisture by the proximity of Africa, and, except in the oases, is therefore thinly peopled. In some degree it partakes of the characteristics both of the marginal belt and of the central area of Euro-Asia. It is mainly devoid of forest, is patched with desert, and is therefore suitable for the operations of the nomad. Dominantly, however, it is marginal, for sea-gulfs and oceanic rivers lay it open to sea-power, and permit of the exercise of such power from it. As a consequence, periodically throughout history, we have here had empires belonging essentially to the marginal series, based on the agricultural populations of the great oases of Babylonia and Egypt, and in free water-communication with the civilized worlds of the Mediterranean and the Indies. But, as we should expect, these empires have been subject to an unparalleled series of revolutions, some due to Scythian, Turkish, and Mongol raids from Central Asia, others to the effort of the Mediterranean peoples to conquer the overland ways from the western to the eastern ocean. Here is the weakest spot in the girdle of early civilizations, for the isthmus of Suez divided sea-power into Eastern and Western, and the arid wastes of Persia advancing from Central Asia to the Persian gulf gave constant opportunity for nomad-power to strike home to the ocean edge, dividing India and China, on the one hand, from the Mediterranean world on the other. Whenever the Babylonian, the Syrian, and the Egyptian oases were weakly held, the steppe-peoples could treat the open tablelands of Iran and Asia Minor as forward posts whence to strike through the Punjab into India, through Syria into Egypt, and over the broken bridge of the Bosphorus and Dardanelles into Hungary. Vienna stood in the gateway of Inner Europe, withstanding the nomadic raids, both those which came by the direct road through the Russian steppe, and those which came by the loop way to south of the Black and Caspian seas.

Here we have illustrated the essential difference between the Saracen and the Turkish controls of the Nearer East. The Saracens were a branch of the Semitic race, essentially peoples of the Euphrates and Nile and of the smaller oases of Lower Asia. They created a great empire by availing themselves of the two mobilities permitted by their land—that of the horse and camel on the one hand, that of the ship on the other. At different times their fleets controlled both the Mediterranean as far as Spain, and the Indian ocean to the Malay islands. From their strategically central position between the eastern and western oceans, they attempted the conquest of all the marginal lands of the Old World, imitating Alexander and anticipating Napoleon. They could even threaten the steppe land. Wholly distinct from Arabia as from Europe, India, and China were the Turanian pagans from the closed heart of Asia, the Turks who destroyed the Saracen civilization.

Mobility upon the ocean is the natural rival of horse and camel mobility in the heart of the continent. It was upon navigation of oceanic rivers that was based the Potamic stage of civilization, that of China on the Yangtse, that of India on the Ganges, that of Babylonia on the Euphrates, that of Egypt on the Nile. It was essentially upon the navigation of the Mediterranean that was based what has been described as the Thalassic stage of civilization, that of the Greeks and Romans. The Saracens and the Vikings held sway by navigation of the oceanic coasts.

The all-important result of the discovery of the Cape road to the Indies was to connect the western and eastern coastal navigations of Euro-Asia, even though by a circuitous route, and thus in some measure to neutralize the strategical advantage of the central position of the steppe-nomads by pressing upon them in rear. The revolution commenced by the great mariners of the Columbian generation endowed Christendom with the widest possible mobility of power, short of a winged mobility. The one and continuous ocean enveloping the divided and insular lands is, of course, the geographical condition of ultimate unity in the command of the sea, and of the whole theory of modern naval strategy and policy as expounded by such writers as Captain Mahan and Mr. Spencer Wilkinson. The broad political effect was to reverse the relations of Europe and Asia, for whereas in the Middle Ages Europe was caged between an impassable desert to south, an unknown ocean to west, and icy or forested wastes to north and north-east, and in the east and south-east was constantly threatened by the superior mobility of the horsemen and camelmen, she now emerged upon the world, multiplying more than thirty-fold the sea surface and coastal lands to which she had access, and wrapping her influence round the Euro-Asiatic land-power which had hitherto threatened her very existence. New Europes were created in the vacant lands discovered in the midst of the waters, and what Britain and Scandinavia were to Europe in the earlier time, that have America and Australia, and in some measure even Trans-Saharan Africa, now become to Euro-Asia. Britain, Canada, the United States, South Africa, Australia, and Japan are now a ring of outer and insular bases for sea-power and commerce, inaccessible to the land-power of Euro-Asia.

But the land power still remains, and recent events have again increased its significance. While the maritime peoples of Western Europe have covered the ocean with their fleets, settled the outer continents, and in varying degree made tributary the oceanic margins of Asia, Russia has organized the Cossacks, and, emerging from her northern forests, has policed the steppe by setting her own nomads to meet the Tartar nomads. The Tudor century, which saw the expansion of Western Europe over the sea, also saw Russian power carried from Moscow through Siberia. The eastward swoop of the horsemen across Asia was an event almost as pregnant with political consequences as was the rounding of the Cape, although the two movements long remained apart.

It is probably one of the most striking coincidences of history that the seaward and the landward expansion of Europe should, in a sense, continue the ancient opposition between Roman and Greek. Few great failures have had more far-reaching consequences than the failure of Rome to Latinize the Greek. The Teuton was civilized and Christianized by the Roman, the Slav in the main by the Greek. It is the Romano-Teuton who in later times embarked upon the ocean; it was the Graeco-Slav who rode over the steppes, conquering the Turanian. Thus the modern land-power differs from the sea-power no less in the source of its ideals than in the material conditions of its mobility.[*]

In the wake of the Cossack, Russia has safely emerged from her former seclusion in the northern forests. Perhaps the change of greatest

---

[*] This statement was criticized in the discussion which followed the reading of the paper. On reconsidering the paragraph, I still think it substantially correct. Even the Byzantine Greek would have been other than he was had Rome completed the subjugation of the ancient Greek. No doubt the ideals spoken of were Byzantine rather than Hellenic, but they were not Roman, which is the point.

intrinsic importance which took place in Europe in the last century was the southward migration of the Russian peasants, so that, whereas agricultural settlements formerly ended at the forest boundary, the centre of the population of all European Russia now lies to south of that boundary, in the midst of the wheat-fields which have replaced the more western steppes. Odessa has here risen to importance with the rapidity of an American city.

A generation ago steam and the Suez canal appeared to have increased the mobility of sea-power relatively to land-power. Railways acted chiefly as feeders to ocean-going commerce. But trans-continental railways are now transmuting the conditions of land-power, and nowhere can they have such effect as in the closed heart-land of Euro-Asia, in vast areas of which neither timber nor accessible stone was available for road-making. Railways work the greater wonders in the steppe, because they directly replace horse and camel mobility, the road stage of development having here been omitted.

In the matter of commerce it must not be forgotten that ocean-going traffic, however relatively cheap, usually involves the fourfold handling of goods—at the factory of origin, at the export wharf, at the import wharf, and at the inland warehouse for retail distribution; whereas the continental railway truck may run direct from the exporting factory into the importing warehouse. Thus marginal ocean-fed commerce tends, other things being equal, to form a zone of penetration round the continents, whose inner limit is roughly marked by the line along which the cost of four handlings, the oceanic freight, and the railway freight from the neighbouring coast, is equivalent to the cost of two handlings and the continental railway freight. English and German coals are said to compete on such terms midway through Lombardy.

The Russian railways have a clear run of 6000 miles from Wirballen in the west to Vladivostok in the east. The Russian army in Manchuria is as significant evidence of mobile land-power as the British army in South Africa was of sea-power. True, that the Trans-Siberian railway is still a single and precarious line of communication, but the century will not be old before all Asia is covered with railways. The spaces within the Russian Empire and Mongolia are so vast, and their potentialities in population, wheat, cotton, fuel, and metals so incalculably great, that it is inevitable that a vast economic world, more or less apart, will there develop inaccessible to oceanic commerce.

As we consider this rapid review of the broader currents of history, does not a certain persistence of geographical relationship become evident? Is not the pivot region of the world's politics that vast area of Euro-Asia which is inaccessible to ships, but in antiquity lay open to the horse-riding nomads, and is to-day about to be covered with a network of railways? There have been and are here the conditions of a mobility of military and economic power of a far-reaching and yet

THE NATURAL SEATS OF POWER.

Pivot area—wholly continental. Outer crescent—wholly oceanic. Inner crescent—partly continental, partly oceanic.

limited character. Russia replaces the Mongol Empire. Her pressure on Finland, on Scandinavia, on Poland, on Turkey, on Persia, on India, and on China, replaces the centrifugal raids of the steppemen. In the world at large she occupies the central strategical position held by Germany in Europe. She can strike on all sides and be struck from all sides, save the north. The full development of her modern railway mobility is merely a matter of time. Nor is it likely that any possible social revolution will alter her essential relations to the great geographical limits of her existence. Wisely recognizing the fundamental limits of her power, her rulers have parted with Alaska; for it is as much a law of policy for Russia to own nothing over seas as for Britain to be supreme on the ocean.

Outside the pivot area, in a great inner crescent, are Germany, Austria, Turkey, India, and China, and in an outer crescent, Britain, South Africa, Australia, the United States, Canada, and Japan. In the present condition of the balance of power, the pivot state, Russia, is not equivalent to the peripheral states, and there is room for an equipoise in France. The United States has recently become an eastern power, affecting the European balance not directly, but through Russia, and she will construct the Panama canal to make her Mississippi and Atlantic resources available in the Pacific. From this point of view the real divide between east and west is to be found in the Atlantic ocean.

The oversetting of the balance of power in favour of the pivot state, resulting in its expansion over the marginal lands of Euro-Asia, would permit of the use of vast continental resources for fleet-building, and the empire of the world would then be in sight. This might happen if Germany were to ally herself with Russia. The threat of such an event should, therefore, throw France into alliance with the over-sea powers, and France, Italy, Egypt, India, and Corea would become so many bridge heads where the outside navies would support armies to compel the pivot allies to deploy land forces and prevent them from concentrating their whole strength on fleets. On a smaller scale that was what Wellington accomplished from his sea-base at Torres Vedras in the Peninsular War. May not this in the end prove to be the strategical function of India in the British Imperial system? Is not this the idea underlying Mr. Amery's conception that the British military front stretches from the Cape through India to Japan?

The development of the vast potentialities of South America might have a decisive influence upon the system. They might strengthen the United States, or, on the other hand, if Germany were to challenge the Monroe doctrine successfully, they might detach Berlin from what I may perhaps describe as a pivot policy. The particular combinations of power brought into balance are not material; my contention is that from a geographical point of view they are likely to rotate round the pivot state, which is always likely to be great, but with limited mobility as compared with the surrounding marginal and insular powers.

I have spoken as a geographer. The actual balance of political power at any given time is, of course, the product, on the one hand, of geographical conditions, both economic and strategic, and, on the other hand, of the relative number, virility, equipment, and organization of the competing peoples. In proportion as these quantities are accurately estimated are we likely to adjust differences without the crude resort to arms. And the geographical quantities in the calculation are more measurable and more nearly constant than the human. Hence we should expect to find our formula apply equally to past history and to present politics. The social movements of all times have played around essentially the same physical features, for I doubt whether the progressive desiccation of Asia and Africa, even if proved, has in historical times vitally altered the human environment. The westward march of empire appears to me to have been a short rotation of marginal power round the south-western and western edge of the pivotal area. The Nearer, Middle, and Far Eastern questions relate to the unstable equilibrium of inner and outer powers in those parts of the marginal crescent where local power is, at present, more or less negligible.

In conclusion, it may be well expressly to point out that the substitution of some new control of the inland area for that of Russia would not tend to reduce the geographical significance of the pivot position. Were the Chinese, for instance, organized by the Japanese, to overthrow the Russian Empire and conquer its territory, they might constitute the yellow peril to the world's freedom just because they would add an oceanic frontage to the resources of the great continent, an advantage as yet denied to the Russian tenant of the pivot region.

————

Before the reading of the paper, the PRESIDENT said : We are always very glad when we can induce our friend Mr. Mackinder to address us on any subject, because all he says to us is sure to be interesting and original and valuable. There is no necessity for me to introduce so old a friend of the Society to the meeting, and I will therefore at once ask him to read his paper.

After the reading of the paper, the PRESIDENT said : We hope that Mr. Spencer Wilkinson will offer some criticism on Mr. Mackinder's paper. Of course, it will not be possible to avoid geographical politics to a certain extent.

Mr. SPENCER WILKINSON : It would occur to me that the most natural thing and the most sincere thing to say at the beginning is to endeavour to express the great gratitude which, I am sure, every one here feels for one of the most stimulating papers that has been read for a long time. As I was listening to the paper, I looked with regret on some of the space that is unoccupied here, and I much regret that a portion of it was not occupied by the members of the Cabinet, for I gathered that in Mr. Mackinder's paper we have two main doctrines laid down : the first, which is not altogether new—I think it was foreseen some years back in the last century—that since the modern improvements of steam navigation the whole of the world has become one, and has become one political system. I forget the